What People are Saying About the Author's Manifesto for "Allowing Every Person's Natural-Born Potential to Blossom"

"As Founder, Publisher & Editor-in-Chief of an award-winning global media digest, I've had the unique opportunity to curate thousands of essays on topics from across the life, culture, and business spectrum over the past decade-plus. As one of our premier Featured Contributors, Peter has from day one distinguished his works from so many others via his mastery of the written word, and at a time when humanity needs genuine, balanced, perspective. Such authenticity is not only rare but sets a worthy standard for so many others to follow. I and we are proud to be associated with such a fine human being."

Dennis Pitocco, Chief Reimaginator | Award-Winning 360° Nation, USA

"A brilliant, layered, rich, and meaningful pathway to a new paradigm in which trust and inspiration can flourish. Thank you for this thoughtful, thorough writing, this manifesto that resonates in so many ways. May we break with "Command/Control" paradigm and build a "Trust and Inspire" world for humanity and in harmony with the natural world."

Laura Staley, Greater Asheville, North Carolina USA

"Peter Nicholls, I totally love your Manifesto! So many key points and agree with Leslie (Thomas) Flowers, this is a book. I, too, see so much distress and unhappiness because people do not lose themselves in their passion, thus finding themselves. This creates efforts to search for what is already within. My husband and I are about to embark on a new adventure going full time RV living. We love the outdoors and look forward to the simple life, while still engaging in the "work" we do. The best of both worlds. Keep shining your light... the world needs it more now than ever!"

Eileen Bild, Jackson Florida, USA

"This is truly a profound and powerful Manifesto, Peter Nicholls! Yes, it is time, past time to reimagine the workplace. The Seven Keys to Enjoy Being Your True Self is a fabulous foundation. And what if... as we try and rearrange workflow, emotional engagement, think tank modules etc., and the team member likes the old way of doing things, and they are a solid employee. I believe these new models will require an entirely new way to approach the hiring process."

Carolyn Lebanowski, Lisbon, Portugal

"As terrible as COVID-19 has been, it has opened the eyes and minds of so many people that there is far more to life than a paycheck and the realization that no job or title or amount of money is worth a shattered life or working yourself to an early grave."

Frank Zaccari, California, USA

Free to Be Me

Why a Life Ethic is Replacing the Work Ethic

Peter Nicholls

Other Books by Peter Nicholls

Enjoy Being You

Enjoy Being Proud of Who You Are

The Hunger to Grow

Free to Be Me

Why a Life Ethic is Replacing the Work Ethic

Peter Nicholls

DoctorZed
Publishing
www.doctorzed.com

Copyright © 2023 by Peter Nicholls

All rights reserved. No part of this book may be used or reproduced by any means, graphic, electronic, or mechanical, including photocopying, recording, taping or by any information storage retrieval system without the written permission of the publisher except in the case of brief quotations embodied in critical articles and reviews.

Books may be ordered through booksellers or by contacting: www.australiaspeoplegardener.life

ISBN: 978-0-6457955-4-7 (hc)
ISBN: 978-0-6457955-5-4 (sc)
ISBN: 978-0-6457955-6-1 (ebk)

A CiP number for this title can be found at the National Library of Australia.

Cover image tree branch © Olivier Le Moal | Dreamstime

Because of the dynamic nature of the Internet, any web addresses or links contained in this book may have changed since publication and may no longer be valid. The views expressed in this work are solely those of the author. The author does not dispense financial advice or prescribe the use of any technique as a form of guarantee for financial or business viability without the advice of a qualified financial advisor, either directly or indirectly. The intent of the author is only to offer information of a general nature to help you in your business. In the event you use any of the information in this book for yourself or your business, which is your constitutional right, the author and the publisher assume no responsibility for your actions.

.

rev. date 15/06/2023

Contents

Foreword — viii
Acknowledgements — x
A Note About the Traditional Work Ethic — xi
Life's Transitions — xii

Introduction	1
Chapter 1: It Had to Happen	5
Chapter 2: The Rise and Fall of the Work Wall	13
Chapter 3: The View from the Other Side	25
Chapter 4: The Prison of Limited Beliefs	33
Chapter 5: Free to Be Me	43
Chapter 6: The Life Development Ethic	47
Chapter 7: The Natural Leap of Faith	57
Chapter 8: Better for Business	63
Chapter 9: Enjoy Loving the Person You Are	71
Chapter 10: The Global Dream	73
Chapter 11: To Read On, or Not	75
Chapter 12: Enjoyment is a Serious Issue	77
Epilogue	87
Appendices	90
End Notes	104
About Peter Nicholls	106

Foreword

"Running a marathon but sprinting all the way."

For me, no other phrase in this book better encapsulates the feeling of our "life of work" than this one – a marathon which ended temporarily when the Covid-19 pandemic forced us all to stop suddenly and re-assess.

Fortunately for us all, Peter Nicholls has been reassessing what our lives are all about for many years, and this work is the product of that thinking.

Peter places the enjoyment factor at the centre of workplace culture. As a consultant and coach, I have seen this idea starting to catch on in the corporate world. Peter's prescription is exactly what is needed to accelerate this idea, in a post-pandemic environment where we have all been rethinking our values and priorities.

I've known Peter for many years. He has a perspective on life which comes from careful thought and a long engagement with – and compassion for – people and the human condition.

Foreword

He is driven by a desire to help people realise their full potential and to enjoy their natural gifts – and thereby to live a life which is not solely driven by commercial imperatives or work factors.

I've done one of Peter's programs. It was a rare chance to stop and reflect – to step out of the marathon and to see myself through the various stages of my life. I was able to see how I'd gotten to where I am now – and also what I had given up to do that. It made me rethink what I want to do with the time I have left in my life, and reminded me to do more of the things in my life that I find most enjoyable.

This book is necessary work. It will make an immediate change in your life, and will continue to make changes in the lives of other for many years – it is truly a legacy for generations to come.

*No-one else can live the rest of our lives for us –
it is all in our own hands.*

I'm very grateful to Peter for sharing his thinking, experience and humanity, and for making it available for the rest of us. You will be too.

Gary Edwards,
Executive Communication Coach,
National President Professional Speakers Australia

Acknowledgements

The content of this book is the product of my fifty years professionally promoting the enjoyment of life. Of those who have helped me over the years, three people stand out.

Sally A. Curtis. Sally has so often helped me clarify my business focus. Her caring suggestions have always kept me moving forward. Her caring, deep friendship has always buoyed me whenever life gets me down.

Gary Edwards has similarly been a staunch ally and true business friend. He has brought meaning and clarity to my efforts in demonstrating to clients the benefits of enjoyment - in business and personal lives. The "7 Key Features of Enjoying Being Your True Self" model is the product of Gary's visualising skills.

John Gallehawk. For 20 years, John has been my best friend and my toughest critic. I owe so much of the content and development of this book to John's wise words, and his deep, life-long experience in the book trade.

A Note About the Traditional Work Ethic

This book does not argue the work ethic should be replaced by what I call a life ethic. The shift is already happening - globally. The reasons why are explained in the following chapters. I have received widespread agreement and support for this transition.

I see the traditional work ethic as having for centuries *publicly perceived* enjoyment as opposite to work. In the workplace, enjoyment has been seen to have no value – even being detrimental – to financial success and economic development.

The new ethic embraces enjoyment as an essential ingredient not only to financial success but to the very reasons why each of us is here today.

Work – including hard work – is now recognised as only one of many factors in the desire for a life of personal and financial success.

Life's Transitions

You are facing your most important life transition, simply because it's happening right now.

You may even feel as though your life is in foreign territory. Our states of mind can act as friends or foes.

Which of the following apply to you at this time?

- Courage or fear?
- Clarity or complexity?
- Certainty or uncertainty?
- Positivity or negativity?
- Purposefulness or aimlessness?
- Expansiveness or insularity?
- Curiosity or apathy?

Only you can determine the path you are on and the direction you want to go. The "what?" and "how?" questions can wait.

Life's Transitions

For now, the "why?" questions are the most important. Why are you making this transition? Why are you at this crossroads? Why is it important to you to make this change at this particular time?

The answers aren't "out there". The answers aren't even in this book. The answers have always been within you. This book takes you back to the basics of who you are, so that you can access and explore your unique, natural-born gifts and passions. These are the strengths you can draw on to plan and create your best life yet.

> *I believe every person was born to live their best life, using their talents and following their passions to achieve their unique potential.*
>
> *Working for the sake of it is not fulfilling. Working with a passion to use and develop one's talents and gifts in order to achieve a desired outcome can be hard. But it's also energising, life-enhancing, and valuable.*

Introduction

Flying in the Face of Human Nature

Like every other living creature on this planet, we were born for a reason. An acorn, for example, grows to become an oak tree. It doesn't stop growing at any pre-determined age. It continues to grow until its eventual demise. We tend to speak of trees ageing, rather than being old. The more a tree ages, the more likely we are to speak of it as being 'significant'.

Nor should we think of the oak standing there doing nothing. It is the epitome of constant energy and activity on its life journey of growing, flourishing, and blossoming.

Try standing with your back against any established tree. Feel the very power of its energy roaring up the trunk from its roots, and spreading to support each leaf's search for light. Its strengths are not in what we can see but in what we cannot see. As a rule of thumb, its root system is one and a half times the depth and width of what we see.

This gives the tree two vital life-giving strengths:

1. The stability to withstand the winds and storms of life
2. The capacity for its root system to search far and wide for the resources that drive the tree's growth.

A tree does not grow alone. Every type of flora and fauna within an ecosystem depends on reciprocal strength and support for its continued survival.

The acorn can only become an oak: it cannot become an apple tree. We humans, however, have been taught for centuries to forget why we were born and to act like the acorn that is told to become an apple tree. No wonder we have become stressed to the eyeballs!

The world has always had leaders who have the power to tell masses of followers what to do. The Industrial Revolution successfully set business principles that put money and profit first. Workers were placed in the role of machines, to be manipulated and discarded as best suited the economic requirements determined by business leaders.

There was little change until the turn of the 21st Century, when technology-driven changes started to put immense pressure on the system. Stress became the number one cost of labour, bordering on burnout and the deterioration of mental health. The leaders were concerned, but life had to go on.

Until now. Not as a result of Covid-19 itself, but because of the global impact of keeping people locked down at home, in some instances for months at a time. Uncertainty and confusion abounded, as no one knew how or when we would get through this change. One thing became certain—we were never going to be able to get back to the way things were before the pandemic.

Instead, people began to recognise that they want a new way of approaching life. One based, in effect, on natural principles that encourage us to grow, flourish, and blossom, each in our own way, to achieve personal goals and to serve the common good. It's a principle I had observed and advocated since the 1970's as a recreation development professional.

Being passionate about one's favourite recreation and sporting interests gave participants an opportunity to taste their best life, even if it was only on the weekends.

From 2003, as a life enjoyment mentor, business managers couldn't see the value of my ideas. Enjoyment was seen as a soft skill unrelated to the rigours of business and unable to be measured in dollar terms. At best, I was told, "Peter, perhaps you are ahead of the times."

I was! Change is now happening. It is time to seize the day and put into words the dream I have held for all those years. In August 2022, I wrote and published *A Manifesto for Allowing Every Person's Natural-born Potential to Blossom*.

Many readers said, "Peter, this needs to become a book."

I do hope you enjoy my response to their urgings. This book differs in that it sees the role of work from the enjoyment of life side of the 'work ethic wall' that was built to protect the 'purity' of work.

Chapter 1

It Had to Happen

Will any of us ever forget?

For me, it was the first week in February 2020. Life as we knew it screamed to a halt, literally overnight. The government had announced a rapidly moving virus known as Covid-19 that had come out of Wuhan, China. It was spreading everywhere, and it was serious. Being over 60—which placed me in the most vulnerable age group—my daughter and daughter-in-law urged me to "Buy up big at the supermarket and stay home for a month!"

No country was excluded, no person was immune. The world had literally shut down. Except for nature's fauna and flora. Animals wondered where everyone had gone. Nature was free to flourish without the hindrances imposed on it by the demands of society. Within weeks people were agreeing how much healthier and cleaner the world was looking with people out of the way. It was the strongest indication yet of the damage people are doing to the natural world.

We were dumbstruck. What had just happened? How long would it go on for? How soon could we get back to the way things were? Absolutely no one in the world had an answer, nor did anyone know how to treat the virus.

It was eerie. A time of global silence… a silence totally alien to the usually hustling, bustling world of human chaos. Ghost cities everywhere. Interestingly, people began to notice the roses, real and proverbial, that they hadn't stopped to smell for years. Sights and sounds and smells that we suddenly realised were always there but which we had rarely noticed.

It was as if the world was suddenly exhausted. We had been running a marathon but sprinting all the way.

The first thing to do was to get things organised at home. Issues like schooling the children, getting exercise, setting up a space as a home office, entertaining the kids, entertaining the adults, lots of Netflix, and plenty of alcohol on hand to ease the pain. Anything to stop us from going stir crazy. This might last for months. The local park became the prison exercise yard. We were allowed to leave our cell for an hour a day.

"Parks are keeping us sane," the cry went up.

This was music to my ears, having worked as a parks and recreation planner for 25 years. Prior to lockdowns, parks were seen by many people as being wasted space that had great developmental value and potential, because they were in prime locations. I had been a very vocal "keep your hands off the parks" advocate throughout my recreation-planning career. I am just as hot on the subject now. Has public opinion about parks improved since then? I fear people forget very quickly. Land is a finite resource and public infrastructure demands grow daily. Hopefully, parks will still be around come the next pandemic!

What to do to get through this seemed to break down into three phases:

1. What to do immediately—individually, locally, and globally. Can we all work from home, including the bosses? Basic survival issues quickly emerged including brawls over toilet paper, hand sanitiser, and basic food supplies.

2. The next phase would be in the medium term. How long would it be before we could make some plans for the coming months?

3. The third phase was too obscure to think about yet. What would we look to be doing in future years if things didn't get back to 'normal'?

We are the children of a world of systems built over many generations, based around work, money and success. We can't live without our daily structure, particularly in our working lives: the demands of our jobs, of management, of organisational systems, and of clients. In those early days of lockdown, we had no structure. New systems had to be made. How and by whom would new structures be decided?

No one was in control. Chief executives and staff alike were questioning their own life circumstances. It was like organisation charts had become a single flat line with everyone from top to bottom facing the same work and personal life issues. We were not just all in it together in the fight to beat the virus. We were all in it together to work out how we were going to move forward in our way of living.

We have always proved to be a resilient lot. As the months passed, people realised we were never going to go back to pre-Covid-19 days. And really, who wanted to? By nature, we want to keep moving forward in life and work. As the lockdown weeks passed, we started to think about what a rat-race life we had been living, how much we had been chasing our tails, unable to look much beyond Friday. Is that the sort of life we would like to go back to? We decided we rather liked this idea of thinking for ourselves and reconsidering where we wanted to go. We had a chance to breathe, think, and make plans—plans we hadn't had the time to even think about before.

We were getting back to the basics of our human nature: human 'beings' instead of human 'doings'. Three years later, it became possible to reflect that the pandemic did more than stop everything. It allowed us the pause to take a long look at ourselves, individually, in communities, and globally. The stage was set for a shift in human thinking.

It's here that I started to get excited, wearing my life enjoyment mentor hat. Back in 2001, I had written my first book, *Enjoy Being You – How Leisure Can Help You Become the Person You Want to Be*. In those first months of lockdown, I decided to quote some of the more popular passages from that book on my social media platforms. The reactions completely overwhelmed me. Those three words "enjoy being you" had struck a chord with readers – "enjoy being the person I want to be, doing the things I love doing and perhaps doing them in a different job serving a different cause".

People indeed had begun to enjoy making their own decisions—or at least making known what they wanted or needed. Working from home, flexible working conditions, getting to like the local neighbourhood they had bypassed for years on their way to the CBD. People were starting to like the sense of freedom to say what they thought, and to ask for conditions that previously would have been dismissed out of hand by the powers that be. The desire to find purpose was taking root, rather than simply trying to fit into a set of work rules.

What I had been saying for almost 50 years was starting to be seen as the way forward—not because of me, but as a result of this massive change in world thinking. The greatest shift since the Industrial Revolution was taking place before our very eyes. It makes for a juicy conspiracy theory... did someone in China know what the power of a pandemic might do to solve the world's problems?

If they did, they could not have imagined the degree of impact it was going to have on everything we do.

Chapter 2

The Rise and Fall of the Work Wall

"Work is the way to salvation... idle hands are the work of the devil!"

So decreed the pundits of the 16th century. Trump-like, a high wall was created, separating the purity of hard work from anything else in life.

The factory owners of the Industrial Revolution happily picked up the message and ran with it. It has since been the expectation – until now.

The pressures and stresses of 21st Century living shook the wall to its foundations. The changes imposed, as a result of Covid-19, finished the job.

The wall has gone and work rightly becomes just one (albeit still important) part of the personal growth mindset that we continue to develop throughout our lives.

Traditional Thinking.

We have had a problem of 19th Century thinking in a 21st Century world. We have been living by what I call the 'Seven Deadly Signs of Work'. The thinking perpetuated by these signs is that:

- Our lives centre around hard work
- Soft skills and mental illness are signs of weakness
- Money is the sole means to success
- Enjoyment is a waste of time that could be devoted to work
- Devotion to work comes before devotion to family
- Stress from hard work is a badge of honour—wear it with pride
- Our identity lasts only for our working lives

The work ethic dominated more than just our work. It created public perceptions of:

- Life being divided into three phases—preparation for paid employment, paid employment, and life after paid employment

- People who aren't in paid employment as being 'less than' working people
- Retirement from paid employment as equating to retirement from life
- A bell-curve lifecycle, peaking at midlife and sliding downhill from there
- Ageism
- A need for education to focus on paid employment, not on life

Of course, we don't talk about 'paid employment'. We talk about 'work'. But there are many different kinds of work, and reducing the assumed meaning to paid employment means that anything which falls outside of that is disregarded as being of less importance. However, the dictionary defines work as 'be engaged in physical or mental activity in order to achieve a result'. There is no mention of money, life success, or the need for work to be stressful.

We live in the Information Age, when change can be rapid and dramatic. We need no longer feel bound by 'we've always done it that way' thinking. The thinking now is often 'if it ain't broke, break it!' We realised there was no over-riding principle telling us how we should respond to the after-effects of the lockdowns. We needed to make our own individual decisions, based on our own skills, talents and wishes. Decisions that could honour true progress, and the health and wellbeing of self and others. True 21st Century progress demands individual and collective freedom to maximise the full range of natural human potential.

Pre-pandemic, research indicated that up to 70% of employees were not feeling engaged in their work. People today are reconsidering their aims in life and their 'place in the sun' in this emerging new world. Post-pandemic, we started to hear about the 'Great Resignation', or 'Great Realignment', in which millions of people began voting with their feet. This was a strong indicator that workers were seeking a greater sense of purpose in their lives.

Flying under the radar is the OECD Better Life Index (www.oecdbetterlifeindex.org/). All OECD countries officially maintain this index. It measures each country's annual progress in terms of more than money, capturing annual statistics on housing, employment, income, community, education, environment, civic engagement, health, life education, safety, and work-life balance.

These statistics may be useful in government decision-making. However, the economic factor continues to be the prime indicator used to determine the state of human progress and wellbeing. Yet there is plenty of evidence that money is not the driver of wellbeing, and this is being supported by the reactions of workers who now realise that life purpose is driven by many factors, of which money is just one.

Governments need to take a closer look at the potential of the Better Life Index information.

The Uncertain Future of Work

Power is increasingly in the hands of the worker. Employees are making their wishes known about key issues such as work flexibility, professional development, and mental health needs. Hierarchical organisation charts are rapidly reshaping, and in some cases even flattening, as the highest and lowest paid workers realise we are all in it together in lots more ways than battling a pandemic.

Some observers are even questioning the level of interest in working. People are thinking for themselves about the future of work in terms of personal priorities. We want to feel we are working for a cause—be it an ethical cause, environmental, or other cause that fits with personal skills, interests, and personal life goals.

Many workers are reportedly no longer prepared to work outside of standard hours, and certainly not if they are not going to be paid to do so. People are increasingly questioning what is important in their personal lives and where work fits within the framework of priorities. Don't get me wrong—work will always be the core of progressive living, it's just a question of why we work and where it fits into our personal life priorities.

One thing is becoming very clear. Working for the sake of working is no longer seen as the pinnacle of a fulfilling life. Having a passion and developing one's talents and gifts to achieve a desired outcome can be hard work. But it's the sort of hard work that is energising, life enhancing and valuable. This kind of work generates the positive stress on which we thrive, rather than the negative stress of working for the sake of it, which widely leads to health problems and burnout.

All of this adds credence to recognising our freedom to choose what gives each of us our best life, allowing our essential natural-born gifts to flow and be valued in the cause of true human progress.

The following diagram outlines the deeper desire for overall human progress in the future:

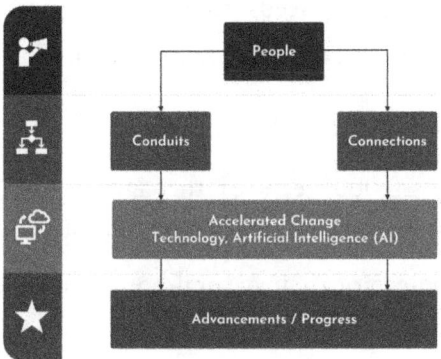

The Future of Work

1. People have a natural yearning to be creative, imaginative, curious, challenged, passionate, and fulfilled
2. People want to connect with positive like-minded people, in order to share and achieve outcomes of common interest
3. People like structures and systems which connect them with others to achieve an agreed purpose
4. There is a human need to effectively manage the rapid change of the Information Age, including the growth and use of Artificial Intelligence
5. Progress needs to advance in a way that improves the wellbeing of people and nature

Distancing Ourselves from Nature

For the 10,000 years of the agrarian era, people based their lives and growth around the use and development of their natural-born talents and gifts. Our connection and relationship to nature were central to our way of living.

We have turned the role of nature from being the centre of the world's health and wellbeing to a means of feeding economic hunger. Artificiality may be bringing people perceived material success, and comfortable living and working conditions. However, our long-term emotional strength, personal development, and wellbeing still depend on our natural state of being.

My background as a parks and leisure professional has taught me how much people love and need to be outdoors in nature. It's time to remember we are partners with nature, not its master.

We have an innate desire to connect with nature in any way we can. I ask my workshop group attendees to describe any recent experience they have enjoyed. In most cases they recount stories about being outdoors in nature.

We feel as though we have come home whenever we get away from the concrete jungles to spend time in nature.

Education

Malala Yousafzai, the youngest person to win the Nobel Peace Prize, took to the stage during the opening ceremony of the 2022 Commonwealth Games and spoke about the importance of education, saying, *"Tonight, teams from 72 countries and territories join the people of Birmingham to celebrate friendship across borders. As we watch the incredible athletes of the Commonwealth Games, remember that every child deserves the chance to reach their full potential and pursue their wildest dreams."*

This way of thinking gives us the freedom to focus on our natural talents and potential, to develop life strategies and bespoke programs to develop them, and to feel encouraged and supported in reaching our goals!

People have long pleaded that education systems are still focused on producing workers, with a factory-line mentality. There is a need to build a greater sense of enjoyment in creativity into the education systems of most countries.

Education is a crucial starting point for people to use their natural gifts to live fulfilling lives. It becomes a shared issue between education systems, parents, and business advocates—all of whom have a significant influence on the decisions of young people during the formative years of their lives.

By taking a round table approach involving educators, parents, and business advocates, young people can be assisted in coming to terms with:

- What they love doing
- What is valuable about their abilities
- What makes them different from other people

It's already standard marketing practice for businesses to focus on the ways in which they are different from their competitors. It is a principle every young person needs to focus on, if they are truly going to enjoy their best life.

This raises an interesting point. Many successful people sidestepped formal education. They are people who learned from the 'school of hard knocks' or who 'dragged themselves up by the bootstraps'. Many successful people simply didn't like school and were regarded as failures because they didn't fit the education mould.

Those people know what education for life means. It means developing skills that enable you to survive the rough and tumble of life. These are the people that need to be part of writing the 21st Century education program, encouraging people to learn the skills that will allow them to grow into the person they were born to be.

What greater joy could there be?

The education system cannot be left to slowly evolve. We have been talking about it for years. People who have succeeded in life, in spite of the education system, need to be invited to help re-write the education rulebook now.

Chapter 3

The View from the Other Side

For half a century I have been working on the 'wrong side' of the work wall, employed in what traditionalists would regard as 'not a real job'. Being on the wrong side of the wall has given me highly valuable insights into peoples' work, life, and growth.

I started work in the late 1950's, when life was far more predictable than it is today. I had no particular ambitions. When I left school, my father found me a government desk job through a friend. I proceeded to progress through life, faithfully performing my role and getting steady promotions. I commuted daily in crowded, peak hour suburban trains to and from the Melbourne CBD in my grey suit, white shirt, and tie. I clocked on and off at precise times.

I soon became financially prepared for marriage and children. I was respected in my community, content to enjoy my life of predictability, conformity, and uniformity.

I had no issues with the work wall in those days. It looked after me and gave me a comfortable, if not especially exciting, existence. Work was my focus for five days a week, and the rest of my life was limited to the weekends. Where I lived, weekend shopping was limited to Saturday mornings. The theory seemed to be that we were expected to spend our time resting in preparation for the important work of the coming week.

Not that we did stop and rest. Sport and recreational activities abounded. It was as though we were released from prison each weekend, keen to make the most of the few hours that we could call our own, before returning to the workplace on Monday morning. I remember weekends in Australia's capital city, Canberra, which is located within hours of the snowfields. On Friday evenings, the main road through Canberra from Sydney would be packed with cars speeding to the snowfields, the occupants eager to be on the slopes at first light on Saturday. The reverse happened each Sunday evening, as skiers left it until the last shred of daylight had slipped away from the slopes before begrudgingly returning to their cars for the breakneck drive back to Sydney, turning up bleary-eyed at work on Monday morning.

I was 24 when I moved interstate to Canberra. Looking back now, that move was the first of some very significant dots that were to connect me to a very unexpected future.

Most of us seem to view the 'Big 0' ages as key stages, when we wonder about the big picture of our lives. I was 30 when I started wondering why I was here. I clearly remember looking out my office window and thinking to myself, *'Thirty-five more years of this and then the proverbial gold watch. Is that it?'* The search was on for the meaning of life. It would take another four years for the answers to come.

At 34, I experienced a day that would change my life forever. A one-day seminar on the topic of *'Leisure As A Social Problem In The 1980s'*. The seminar was part of a new Federal Government policy that included the establishment of post-graduate courses to train people to manage the issues of what people do when they are not at work. I passed the course with flying colours and became a recreation planner in Adelaide.

People thought I was mad to leave a solid job in a prestigious national government department to follow a seemingly dubious new life, and with a significant drop in pay. However, I knew I had found my purpose.

A recreation profession was first established in Australia in the early 1970s. People questioned if it was 'a real job.' An experienced engineer once asked me, "What does a recreation planner do all day… play tennis?"

Two years later, the same engineer came to me and said, "Peter, I am working on a major water conservation project stretching across much of Adelaide. I would like your advice on the recreation potential of the development."

I had won him over.

As a recreation planner, I worked with people of all ages and backgrounds who were seeking ways of improving the quality of their lives through their recreational interests. This included the use of recreation centres, walking trails, playgrounds, sporting facilities, parks, and rivers.

These people were freely choosing and passionately enjoying creative experiences that brought out the best in them, giving them a sense of challenge and desired outcomes that required planning and goal setting.

They were enjoying living their best life away from work, irrespective of how they felt about their work. They were experiencing personal growth and development in its most natural way.

I learned so much about what these experiences do for mental strength, personal health and wellbeing, skill development, stress management, and work/life harmony.

Dealings with influential authorities were, however, frustratingly difficult. Work was king and recreation simply 'fluffy stuff', for which funding and other public support was seen as being of low importance.

The pressures and stresses of the 21st Century lifestyle have made dramatic inroads into this thinking, both in terms of worker perceptions of the role of paid employment and the search for means of managing prolonged, excessive negative stress. People began desperately looking for ways to increase their enjoyment of life.

Enjoy being the real you, because when you lose yourself in any interest that you enjoy, you find yourself.

These words became the mantra of my 'encore career'. Not that I had in any way planned an encore career. Like all good transitions it was a quirk of fate—one that further deepened my understanding of the benefits of enjoyment.

A business colleague in a large private company had read my book, *Enjoy Being You*. She was leading a team of people who were burning out from the prolonged stress of working overseas. She wanted to change things and asked if I could run a workshop based on my book. I agreed.

Before the workshop, my client and I talked about each member of the group. One, she said, was a loner who rarely talked socially with the others. As expected, he was very quiet during the workshop until we started talking about our leisure interests. He said he loved playing chess. With my encouragement the discussion continued for some minutes. The others were amazed. They had never heard him say so much in one sitting.

At the end the group wanted to supplement my fee with a gift. Guess who did the presentation on behalf of the group? The 'loner'. Not only was an enjoyment workshop for workaholics a brilliant success, some went on to establish their own consultancies, with the enjoyment factor being a key factor in their business culture.

Purpose had found me again. I became a 'Life Enjoyment Mentor'.

Chapter 4

The Prison of Limited Beliefs

Imprisoned by Public Perceptions

The 19th Century perception of work has long influenced our thinking about so many aspects of daily life. The factory systems that were developed during the Industrial Revolution forced workers to be part of the production line. Efforts to improve worker productivity, such as the Elton Mayo Hawthorn Experiments of 1927, were undertaken in the belief that the results could be applied to every worker. It has taken a long time for business to realise we are all individuals. The aftereffects of Covid-19 have dramatically highlighted that fact.

Philosophers make a distinction between perception and fact. Was there really a table in front of me, or did my mind simply perceive it as being there? The proof, of course, would come when I walked into it and barked my shin.

Another example is the story of the blind men feeling the elephant, and each explaining what they thought it was. As each man was touching a different part of the elephant, they each had a different perception of what it was. The man who was touching the tail thought it was a rope, the man who was touching the ear thought it was a leaf, the man who was touching the trunk thought it was a snake and so on.

Pre-Covid-19, when it came to work, we were governed by the perceptions of people who were alive centuries ago, and whose views had become embedded in our minds as facts.

We are now free of their perceptions.

Being your true self allows you to have the confidence to say what you think, no matter what others may be saying or thinking, knowing that what you say is a genuine outer expression of your inner thoughts, feelings, and insights.

Whether or not others agree, they are much more likely to listen with respect for your views when you are being true to yourself.

Conversations become genuinely two-way when the speaker and the listener value the fact that we learn from each other. Listening is not an act of waiting for the other person to take a breath so that we can have our say.

The potential to enjoy being our true selves and living our freely chosen best life can, in this way, become the most important and powerful ingredient in developing a whole new way of thinking.

Freedom from Expectations

Expectations greatly influence our thinking and decision-making. Meeting other's expectations drains us. Pride in our own abilities empowers us. Expectations have become a common source of stress and uncertainty in peoples' lives.

The opposite of self-esteem is the need for validation. What we think other people expect of us is a huge part of seeking validation. This drains our energy, because we can never really know what is in the minds of the people we think have expectations of us. It leads us to create expectations of ourselves—a self-imposed pressure to be someone we are not.

We no longer need to kowtow to the expectations we believe others have. We can also banish the sister to expectations—'should'. 'Could' and 'would' have their place, but 'should' is always an expectation in which one person imposes their views on someone else.

Expectations of self can be okay, provided they are part of our drive to achieve our natural-born potential. In that situation, the drive will come naturally through the energising effect of what we enjoy, rather than through a sense of what we 'should' do.

So many of us live a life we were advised to choose by a person whose authority we once respected. Parents, teachers, past bosses, people who felt they knew best what we should do. Well-intentioned or not, the fact is, their perspective was not necessarily ours.

These authority figures are probably no longer directing your life. Yet their influence may still sit deep in your subconscious every time an important life decision is needed.

The truth is, no one else can live your life for you. It is all in your own hands. Over the years, we come to understand ourselves in greater depth. We accumulate a greater understanding of others too, deepening our perspective, insight, and wisdom.

Like the athlete or the artist, we know what we are good at and what we love doing, so that we are able to develop our natural gifts and make the most of our potential. We are loved not for what we achieve but for backing our natural strengths so that we can live our best lives—for ourselves and for those we love.

We do not need to restrict our thinking to the old range of 'proper jobs'. Creativity and innovation are in demand, and those demands need to be met by people with talent and experience.

Teenagers can continue to dream of becoming an actor, singer, artist, or even a recreation planner. Our children need to feel that we appreciate them as blossoming human beings, whose talents, uniqueness, and dreams are worthy of constant nurturing, support and encouragement.

The End of Ageism?

Being regarded as 'too old' to keep working have relevance in certain contexts, but those contexts are always going to be specific. Someone may legitimately be too old to play professional sport by the time they are thirty.

However, there are many professions where it is possible to keep working well beyond the traditional retirement age.

New thinking about ageing is beginning to surface, as this 2019 statement from the United Nations displays:

"Traditionally the United Nations and most researchers have used measures and indicators of population ageing that are mostly or entirely based on people's chronological age, defining older persons as those 60 or 65 years or

over. However there has been an increasing recognition that the mortality risks, health status, type and level of activity, productivity and other socio-economic characteristics have changed significantly in many parts of the world over the last century and particularly in the last few decades. This has led to the development of alternative concepts and measures to offer a more nuanced perspective of what population ageing means in different contexts." [1]

People have the capacity to maintain a growth mindset from birth to death. They can always enjoy the feeling of having a purposeful role to play in society. We can thereby naturally open up a vastly broader range of ways in which to access human skills, to meet any challenge our future can hold.

The issue of the world's ageing population becomes an asset and an opportunity, rather than a problem. Healthy ageing will become a health prevention factor, overriding the current healthcare model, in which funding priorities have had to focus on making sick people well.

Life is NOT Over... It's Only Half Over

The view of paid employment as the pinnacle of achievement would have us believe that once we reach retirement, we start the downhill slide to oblivion. As a result, as retirement approaches, we can start to experience the mental turmoil of a mid-life crisis.

This can prompt thoughts such as, "I could have made much better decisions if I only I'd known XYZ when I was younger."

Our past then runs up against our future. We fear our working life is drawing to a close and we've blown our chance at having a fulfilling career. Of course, not everybody goes into panic mode, but we all must deal with the perception of that 'bell curve' lifecycle that dominates our thinking, planning, and living.

While we can now expect to live to our 80s and beyond, things haven't changed in the perception of what to do after we leave work. People worry about the amount of money they might need, but few think what they will do after they leave work, beyond leisure activities.

Statistically, if you retire at 60, there is a strong possibility you could have another 30 years of life – half as much again!

As a society, we have trouble recognising the work value of people beyond their mid-40s. This mindset creates the possibility of populations living into their 90's, with workers being drawn only from the 20-40 age group. We need to break this mentality!

We need to recognise that people will continue to have a growth mindset for as long as they stay healthy. Typically, the fact that we are staying healthy and living mentally and physically active lives means we are not only living longer, we want to enjoy a sense of purpose and meaning well into our 80s, and beyond.

However, a shift is happening, and instead of a midlife crisis, many people are now experiencing a 'midlife awakening' where they experience a deepening self-awareness and wisdom that only the years of living can provide.

This opens a whole new perspective on our individual and collective human potential.

Chapter 5

Free to Be Me

When asked how he managed to sculpt his masterpiece, the Statue of David, Michelangelo is said to have replied, "I saw the angel in the marble and I carved until I set him free."

We can see the marble as representing a person's imprisonment within a life that requires them to adhere to the expectations of a world that puts the dollar ahead of the heart. The angel is the self who yearns for the freedom to grow their natural gifts, allowing their unique potential to blossom.

The only person who can be the sculptor is the person looking out at the world through your eyes. That fact is the very essence of your personal power, decisions, control, and choice. In the workplace, the organisation may do all they can to promote mental wellbeing, but the answers are totally centred in each individual person. It's why perceptions, expectations and the concept of 'should' are totally alien to enjoyment and all the benefits that enjoyment brings.

The role of society at all levels is to recognise, value, and extol the natural advantages and benefits of this approach as essential to building a global environment of true, sustained human progress and achievement.

During the pandemic, as lockdown continued, our need to think for ourselves began to flow. We began creating our own expectations and started to enjoy being our true selves. This thinking expanded into an understanding that we are free to choose work we want to do, for people who value our abilities, to serve causes that give us a genuine sense of purpose.

Fear of the unknown and uncertainties about the future have begun to shift. Living the life we were born to enjoy entails becoming self-aware, valuing our individuality, and developing our unique strengths and abilities.

While this may seem straightforward, two of the toughest questions to answer are:

"Who am I?" and "Why am I here?"

The fact that most people define themselves by the work they do is a huge part of the reason so many of us are adamant we never want to retire. However, your profession is merely a snapshot view of your deeper self. And if you are one of the purported 70% of Australians who do not feel engaged in their job, what does that say about your identity?

We need a fresh way of thinking in determining a whole of life definition of our personal identity. Three important questions to consider are:

- What am I good at?
- What do other people value about me?
- What makes me different from everyone else?

While the answers might still not be easy, they help us to appreciate that there is more to our identity than the work we do for part of our lives. We can then feel more purposeful in assessing who we are and why we are here. It often helps to have someone we trust suggest the answers for us. Their answers are often surprisingly accurate.

The Law of Correspondence—one of the 12 Universal Laws—includes the statement: "So within, so without."

This advocates the need to bring our inner self and outer self together as 'oneself'. It also suggests that finding balance and happiness starts from the inside.

Enjoying our best life is all about:

- Connecting the dots (see Chapter 12)
- Investing in ourselves by maximising our natural abilities.
- Embracing the principle of 'Ikigai', which can be simplified as meaning 'the reason to live'. This principle refers to a person's whole life, not just their working life.

Developing and utilising your natural abilities to live your best life and effectively contribute to the needs of the world is a very personal responsibility.

How might you achieve this?

Chapter 6

The Life Development Ethic

While people don't want to retire, they don't want to keep working until they drop from exhaustion. They want to continue doing something of value that makes use of their experience, but possibly in a different area from the one in which they were previously employed.

Societal expectations are still that life after work is for rest and recovery: a reward for years of hard work. This view holds that retirement means putting your feet up and leaving the living of life to others.

Not so! It's okay to take on an 'encore career'. It's natural and normal to continue maintaining and developing the growth mindset.

The new world is one in which we will all be encouraged—indeed have the right—to develop our lives in any way we wish, for as long as our physical and mental capacity allows.

If we enjoy being our true selves and understand our purpose in life, there is a good chance we will live longer, healthier and more active lives. This could well generate a drop in the costs of the current healthcare system industry. The money can then be better used for preventive health measures supporting our new sense of life and purpose.

If we put the principle of work as a duty behind us, we need a replacement principle. The principle of life development promotes the understanding that *every person is born to enjoy their best life by developing their talents and following their passions to allow their natural potential to blossom.*

There are, of course, many people who are already living according to the principle of life development.

A clear illustration is the sportsperson who recognises and pursues the potential of their natural physical and mental abilities. They understand their purpose, goals and opportunities, and are aware of the hurdles they need to overcome in order achieve their dreams.

Self-employed people typically fit this picture as well. They base their lives on developing their natural abilities, with purpose and goal setting along the way to reach their potential. Self-employed people work hard, but they do so because of the passion that drives them, not because other are telling them what they 'should' be doing.

From my experience, I see the principle of life development as encompassing:

- A recognition that personal growth and development is based on enjoying, and improving upon, our talents and passions
- An understanding that personal growth and development continues throughout our lives, be it working for pay or for passion, for as long as the mind remains actively healthy
- An awareness that age brings a depth of understanding, insight, perspective, experience, and wisdom.
- Education systems that are designed to support the principle of life development

- Businesses that recognise that sustainable success is based on encouraging, using, developing and valuing peoples' natural abilities—in all areas of life, not just at work
- True work/life harmony—a healthy relationship between professional and personal development
- The maintenance and enjoyment of a growth mindset throughout a person's lifetime

Living The Life Development Lifecycle

Figure 1 is a simple illustration of the traditional perception of the human lifecycle. It reflects the idea that we mature until some point in the middle of our lives and then go into a state of steady decline until we die.

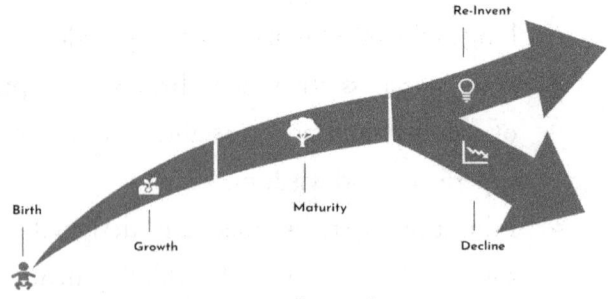

Figure 1: Life Development

In our early adult years we make major life-establishment decisions based on our limited life experience and the influences of older people such as parents and teachers. These can relate to basic life issues such as paid employment, marriage, children, education, a home, and a mortgage.

By 30, we have had enough experience of life to often wonder if our original choices were the right ones. By 40 we are beginning to feel like we are making some sense out of our unique abilities, and considering whether we can do something that makes us feel we are of value to the world and not just going through the motions of a life journey.

By the time of our mid-50s, many people experience a midlife crisis. The perception is that we have reached the pinnacle of life and are heading towards a downward slide towards poor health and death.

As we move into our second half of life we begin to realise what we are good at, what people value about us, and what makes us different from anyone else. We can look forward to many years ahead in which to discover and apply our natural potential. We enjoy a greater sense of self-awareness, and a deeper understanding of where we fit.

The Second Half of Life is The Richest Half of Life

We can change the way we measure our lives. In the same way that we measure age in years, we can measure our lives in the growth of our depth of understanding, insight, experience, knowledge and wisdom. A life measured by these criteria is shown in Figure 2.

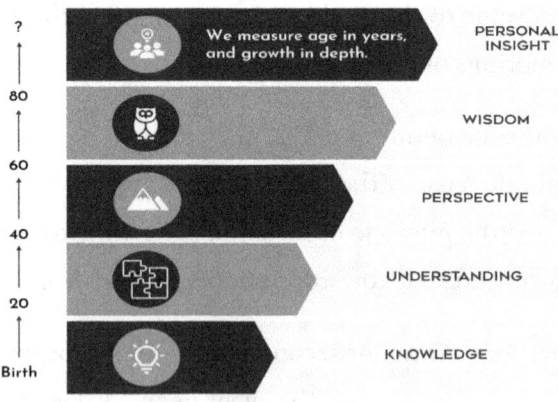

Figure 2: The Second Half of Life

However, even this linear perception does not do justice to the complexity and exponential nature of our second-life growth.

Exponential Growth & Development

Figure 3: Exponential Growth & Development

Exponential growth is cumulative, compounding, even chaotic, rather than linear.

"A huge part of the change in outlook in terms of aging and retirement is based on new understandings of the brain and neuroplasticity - that we can indeed continue to change through choice - and that this is what keeps our brain and mind healthy. Overcoming limiting beliefs about what is possible and having a growth mindset is key! A sense of curiosity to keep exploring and opening up to new experiences. Attitude is everything but it also takes focus, effort and an intrinsic motivation... which not everyone has." [2]

As chaotic or uncertain as the process may be, the one certainty is that it will be based on enjoying using and maximising the natural gifts and passions unique to each of us. Such a foundation opens the way to a path of life we may not have planned.

However, it opens our minds to a direction that seems to fit our wants—often in surprising ways.

The modern world desperately needs to tap into the accumulated potential of this 'explosion' of multi-dimensional human growth and development that naturally occurs in the second half of our lives.

This reality is vital for two reasons of global importance:

1. We live in a world where people aged 60 and over will soon outnumber children aged five and under. In 2030, the first Millennials will start turning 50, and the first Generation X-ers will turn 65. At the end of 2030, the first Baby Boomers will begin turning 85. **There is a great need to see the potential in this, rather than seeing it as a problem.**[3]

2. To end the scourge of ageism— particularly in relation to employment—which is based solely on a person's age.

Chapter 7

The Natural Leap of Faith

There are so many benefits that come from living your best life. Many of them have already been mentioned. The key ones are summarised below.

However, these benefits can only be accessed once you have the mindset to embrace the principle of life development. After all, if you have been working under the thumb of bosses who view work as a duty, you are unlikely to get up tomorrow morning and decide you're no longer going to subscribe to that way of thinking.

Generations of living and working according to other people's expectations and demands have dulled people's sense of initiative and self-belief. To set up one's life on one's own terms then becomes something of a leap of faith. Taking this leap can inspire us to have courage or become something to fear. That is perhaps an issue beyond the realms of this book.

However, there are plenty of positives we can all take forward to do more than survive the changes. Looking at a life centred on the enjoyment factor opens up many positives in how to build a solid future.

Being aware that the world of work and life is dramatically changing gets our minds ready to seriously question not just 'what's next?', but 'what is now possible?'

The shift in power from corporations to individuals is already affecting our daily thinking. It's the first strong indicator that the future is very much in our own hands.

In my first book, *Enjoy Being You,* I talked about the magnificent uncertainty of life. We have always had a say in our future. It's just that now we are being encouraged to think that in this very different new world, we all have something of value to offer.

Your best life allows you to believe in yourself, appreciate who you are, walk tall, and meet people's gaze with warmth and confidence.

Living in a world that recognises, lives by, and promotes success is going to give you all the courage you need to live your best life, allowing you to find and pursue your purpose in life.

In summary, the principle of life development promotes:

The joy of learning with purpose—the mind is actively searching for options, looking for answers, open to new ideas, curious about the bigger picture, and exploring the magic of our imagination.

Energy management over time management—a small amount of time spent enjoying an energising interest sustains energy for much longer than the time of the experience. Regular exposure to energising interests makes for more productive work projects. Burnout becomes a thing of the past.

Stress management and resilience—the more we enjoy what we are doing, at work, home or play, the stronger our ability to deal with stressful life situations.

Positive engagement—we cannot be negative while we are enjoying what we are doing. An accumulation of positive experiences generates a durable positive outlook, including an ability to see beyond problem situations and instead to search for positive answers.

Creativity and innovation—enjoyment activates one's natural abilities and passions, as a result of which we are better able to find original and alternative answers that guide our decisions and choices in new and exciting directions.

Natural problem-solving processes—enjoyment generates a sense of mental calmness, common sense, and clarity about problems we need to address. This provides a natural form of structured thinking, opening the way for us to find better solutions, and to do so more easily.

The confidence to know others will listen to and respect what we say—the more we spend our lives doing things we enjoy, the greater confidence we have in our life learnings. Not only do we find ourselves confidently expressing a point of view, people feel we are worth listening to. They may not always agree with what we say, but what we say will always be respected.

Feeling closely connected with like-minded people—people who enjoy life want to be with other people who share their sense of enthusiasm, passion, and calmness about everything they do. They find themselves spending less time with negative people. Happy communities positively energise each other.

High self-esteem, self-confidence, and self-belief—because we have learned who we are, what we love doing, what other people value about us, and what makes each of us stand out from the crowd.

Chapter 8

Better for Business

Incorporating the enjoyment factor into workplace culture enables businesses to become truly progressive and productive. People, not corporations, create change.

The workplace is already rapidly moving away from the belief that bosses know best and employees follow unquestioningly. We are increasingly seeing higher levels of interaction between employers and employees in efforts to reach new agreements on how best workplaces can operate and produce mutually desired outcomes. Working from home versus working at the office, work flexibility, staff mental health and wellbeing, and resignations.

These are all symptoms of the shifts that are going on. No doubt they will continue for some time yet before any sense of stability is achieved in the way we work and how we conduct business.

The theme 'we are all in it together' continues into the world of work. While changes in the way we work put a huge responsibility on chief executives, life after Covid-19 is as uncertain for them as it is for everyone.

It is through this unsettled process that changes from the principle of work as a duty to the principle of work as life development are gradually being incorporated into workplace cultures, systems, and operations.

For example, the belief that mental health was not a topic for discussion in the workplace resulted in people being reluctant to discuss mental health issues for fear of negative repercussions that spanned the spectrum of everything from being ignored to losing their job. Mental health is now beginning to be recognised by businesses as one of the biggest and most important issues.

Since the focus of this book is on the individual, the following information relates more to how life development is understood, applied, and valued by senior management to maximise staff stability, commitment, engagement, and productivity. In this model, workforces truly become *human* resources.

The principle of life development is based on the importance of management recognising emotion as the glue that binds together the people, the workplace culture, and the purpose of the business.

The most practical and relevant way I can demonstrate the importance of what have traditionally been seen as 'soft skills' is through outlining some of the points from the *7 Keys to Enjoying Being Your True Self*.

These points necessitate recognising and utilising the resources of the individual, with each person being valued for their unique mix of talents, gifts, and developed skills.

Figure 4: 7 Keys to Enjoying Being Your True Self

The Enjoyment Factor and Workplace Culture

- The aim and benefits of the enjoyment factor are about staff feeling satisfied, content, engaged and committed to the organisation and its aims.
- When the enjoyment factor is at the centre of business operations, everything else falls into place.

Connection

Connection is perhaps the most important focus of an enjoyable workplace.

It means two-way communication, both vertically and horizontally, which means listening to hear each other, awareness of what is going on around the workplace, and appreciating that what people say is a genuine reflection of their experience and their perspective of the world.

A Positive Outlook

This isn't about looking at everything in business through rose-coloured glasses. It's about looking beyond problems to the bigger picture, in the search for purposeful solutions.

Talents/Gifts

Each person's unique gifts are needed by someone, somewhere. Some people's gifts see them labelled as geniuses.

Yet everyone has an inner genius wanting to be recognised and developed for outcomes that need their particular gifts. Not everyone recognises their inner genius. It is often someone else who tells them, 'you are a genius' when the person comes up with the answer that somebody wanted.

Great is the leader who can find and extract the inner genius in the people they lead.

Energy

We all love that feeling of good energy in a room or group. Enjoyment generates the energy that drives our personal life and our business life.

The life of each person in the workplace and in the business itself is more about energy management than it is about time management. It's the enjoyment factor in every situation that generates the mental and emotional energy to thrive, grow, and progress. A balanced flow of energy in and energy out is the key to sustained productive output.

Passion

My good friend Charles Kovess, Australia's 'Passion Provocateur', defines passion this way, "Passion is an unlimited source of energy from the soul (or 'spirit', or 'heart') that enables a person to produce extraordinary results. The reason the results are 'extraordinary' is because few people are passionate in their workplace. Passionate people have massive amounts of energy". [4]

The perception of work as a duty saw management regarding the expression of passion by staff as something that needed to be controlled, even repressed, for fear of it getting out of hand. Positively connecting passionate people within an organisation can now be recognised for the asset it is—a key form of energy driving imaginative, creative, productive business.

Continuous Development

Continuous development has major implications for the business sector. The emphasis shifts away from an age-based approach to one of accumulated skills, experiences, depth of understanding human behaviour, insight, perspective, and wisdom. Add to this the likelihood that such recognition will extend the life, health, and value of staff well beyond the current perceptions of staff having a use-by date.

The Whole is Greater than the Sum of its Parts

The cumulative impact of these 7 Keys can be likened to the Big Bang theory. Activation of any one of the seven can trigger a chain reaction of energy generated by all the seven Keys. When a business incorporates the 7 Keys into its workplace culture, there is no limit to the potential output of the business.

In time...

By applying the 7 keys, the following outcomes are likely to be achieved:

- Productivity will boom
- Mental health issues will be monitored and reduced
- Stress will be limited to 'positive stress'
- Conflicts will be reduced and there will be a higher quality of team output
- Personal and corporate goals will be more harmonious, improving staff stability
- The right staff will be attracted to the right jobs.

Chapter 9

Enjoy Loving the Person You Are

Authenticity has become the new black. We are demanding integrity—a quality that goes deeper than words and actions. Integrity comes from within our authentic self.

To fully enjoy experiencing and living our best life depends on knowing, understanding, and loving our authentic self.

Historically, the person we are at work and the person we are after we leave the workplace has battered many of us into living a double life. Many people feel that they leave their true self outside the workplace door, taking no more than the essentials needed for the job. They do what the boss requires and no more, laughter being an out-of-place distraction and personal issues left at home.

This workplace thinking is so deeply embedded that it's no surprise we question how much we truly know, let alone love, our inner self. This is especially true for people whose lives have been dominated by long hours of excessively stressful work to the point where home is merely a place to sleep.

People who work in an organisation that reflects any of the seven deadly signs of the perception of work as a duty are likely to have had their enjoyment dulled.

Under these circumstances, work may dominate most areas of their professional and personal life. This can lead to the belief that being negative is realistic and being positive meaning we do not fully understand the harsh realities of life.

It's a bit like personal relationships. We hear that daunting statement, 'before you can truly love someone else, you need to love yourself'.

In that context we recognise the difference between saying 'I love the person I am' and 'I love myself'. Believing the latter would give you about the same chance of enjoying your best life as it would of getting you the life partner of your dreams.

Chapter 10

The Global Dream

The core of this dream is for people to experience the enjoyment factor in living their best lives. Lives in which we all enjoy creating ripple effects of positive thinking, connecting with like-minded people and sharing productive outcomes through expressing our naturally creative gifts.

There needs to be an understanding of what it means to be self-responsible.

Through self-responsibility, we can all come together and marry those enjoyment factors to make the place, the world, the planet, and our communities better places to live, thrive, and be.

As for the impact on business, a good way to sum up the dream is to go back to the diagram on the future of work.

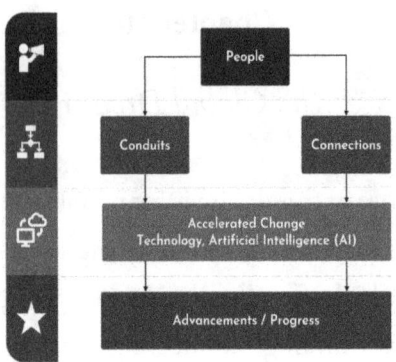

The Future of Work

If everyone based his or her approach to life around the principle of life development, the rest of the system would fall into place. Like-minded people would come together and connect to create businesses and other conduits to make and manage change

The world would be a better, safer, more productive, more natural place. An ideal world in which every person could enjoy living their best life by developing their talents and gifts, follow their passions, and allow their natural potential to blossom.

It all starts with you.

Chapter 11

To Read On, or Not

To help you decide where you are at present, consider which of the following most closely applies to your thinking:

1. You see work as your reason for living, and have few outside interests.

2. You enjoy at least one favourite interest away from work.

3. You have begun questioning your purpose.

4. You feel you are enjoying a harmonious mix of professional and personal interests.

5. You live life with a strong sense of purpose and enjoy developing your natural abilities in your professional and personal life.

If 1 – 3 best fit your thinking at present, you will do well to read on and pay careful attention to the chapter, 'Enjoying Personal Development'

If you relate best to options 4 or 5, the information and ideas in the following chapters will help to further your ongoing quest to embrace your professional and personal interests as seamless components of your best life.

Chapter 12

Enjoyment is a Serious Issue

Our identity is rooted in knowing what we are good at, what people value about us, and what makes us different from everybody else. We find the answers through a deep understanding of what it means to enjoy being our true selves.

Enjoyment is an emotion we tend to gloss over. We tend to decide that we either enjoy an experience or we don't. Yet without the enjoyment factor, we can never truly grow, flourish, or blossom.

No one can tell us what to enjoy. Whether it is at work or in our leisure time, through our enjoyment we are using and expressing gifts unique to each of us. Sometimes we might not even recognise we are doing so. We are just being our true selves using our unique gifts.

Enjoyment is the core of everything that drives our personal growth and development, from birth to death. Enjoyment is the positive part of one's life, no matter what is happening around us. If you are not enjoying life you are living a life of stress. If you are not engaged in your work then you are not enjoying what you are doing. It is draining your energy and potentially exposing you to burnout.

Deeply enjoyable experiences are a source of enrichment and expansion. Enjoyment becomes the energy that drives our lives. It becomes the wind beneath our wings.

Consider the difference between a task you enjoy and a task you don't enjoy. When you enjoy a task, you leap into whatever is required of you, allowing all your creativity and natural gifts to flow. You feel positive, productive, and enthusiastic. You see the task in the context of the bigger picture. You produce a great result.

You may still want to put your best effort into a task you don't enjoy. However, the enthusiasm drops and there's not the same positive creative thinking going into the task. Your productivity level is lower.

The difference in the two tasks is in the presence or absence of the enjoyment factor.

When you enjoy a task, it's as though you have access to a three-phase power source: the energising power when anticipating undertaking the task, the energising effects felt during the task itself, and the reflective enjoyment as you look back on a job well done. Later, you can notice how these good feelings ripple through the rest of the day, and create a more positive outlook as you come to the next task (even if you don't particularly want to do it).

Other benefits from the enjoyed task include:

- The positive perspective you gain from the whole experience.
- The mind operating in search mode, seeking purposeful outcomes, being open to ideas, and exploring different approaches .
- Heightened self-esteem, self-belief and self-confidence.
- Higher retention of information learned during the performance of the task.

Mental Fitness

Any activity we enjoy is valuable in sustaining our mental fitness.

When we lose ourselves in any enjoyable experience, a 'switch on, switch off' process takes place. Our mind becomes absorbed in the positive feelings of the enjoyable activity, and switches off from whatever stresses it was previously focused on. It simply isn't possible to think negatively during an enjoyable experience.

Think of the last time you experienced a simple enjoyment. Remember how it energised you and created a ripple effect that carried into your next activity. Celebrate enjoyable moments regularly and before long you are likely to see life a little more positively. Your resilience may rise and a greater durability to cope with life may begin to develop.

See Appendix 2 for simple suggestions on building enjoyment into your daily life. None of the suggestions are unusual, but they may help you to stay mentally fit.

Leisure Pursuits As Education For Living

Leisure has been wrongly perceived as what to do when there's nothing to do. In truth, a leisure activity is any creative interest you love pursuing purely for its intrinsic satisfaction and enjoyment. It provides creative expression without expectation from anyone else. Such experiences often teach us something new about our own abilities and ourselves.

What we used to see as time off becomes a key opportunity to explore what you can do without having to meet the expectations of others. It's the opportunity to freely express yourself in ways that help you understand how you grow your life.

What more satisfying and valuable education can we get than through expressing our gifts in our own way for our own reasons?

Yes, You Can!

Any experience you create for the sheer enjoyment of doing so unlocks all the following personal development factors in the process of educating yourself to live your best life. Have in mind a favourite interest as you check the following list.

Yes, you can:

- Freely choose to do what you enjoy.
- Be in total control of the whole experience, requirements, expectations, stress levels, and aims.
- Experiment with your own ideas, wishes, and thinking.
- Custom design experiences to suit you.
- Decide your chosen level of desired excellence, whether to do it competitively or socially, alone or with others, and which of your talents or skills to use or test for yourself. You set your own horizon.
- Enjoy the sense of self-empowerment the experience gives you. Take full credit for any outcome you achieve... or learn and profit from what didn't work.
- Pursue the interest:
    o When you want.
    o For as long as you want.

    - o   At the pace you like.
    - o   In the setting of your choice.
    - o   To your chosen level of skill and ability.
- Enjoy the sense of satisfaction you gain from the experience, how good it makes you feel about yourself, how it enriches your life, and improves your health and wellbeing.
- Enjoy a healthy temporary escape from the problems and pressures of life.
- Renew your energy and enthusiasm for living.
- Be childlike again.
- Enjoy the liberating feeling of being your true self.

These experiences become your natural stress manager.

Connecting The Dots

In his Stanford University Commencement speech in 2005, Steve Jobs said, "It was impossible to connect the dots looking forward, but they were very clear when looking back".

He was referring to how certain events in his life were stepping-stones for where he was by 2005.

It can be an illuminating exercise to look back and remember all your enjoyable experiences… to join the dots in your life that have brought you to being the person you are today. And to decide what these experiences tell you about your best self, the person you enjoy being, and the person you want to take forward into the years to come.

The authentic self is the product of every enjoyable experience in your life, including those you can't immediately remember. What parts of your authentic self do you see as being the foundation on which to build the next phase of your life?

Pre-School Years

The power of play is considerable. The dramatic growth that occurs from the time of our birth to the time we start school at the age of five forms most of our basic life-skills, all of which are primarily developed through play.

The principles of play and its links to learning and growth never change. Throughout our school years and into adulthood we continue to learn and grow through play, although perhaps not as dramatically as in our first five years. Every good teacher knows the best way to educate people is to make the process fun.

Youth

For many of us, our youth is spent dreaming of futures we would like to explore. No matter what happened to those dreams, the things we enjoyed in our teenage and young adult years can still tell us a lot about who we are now and who we might still want to be. Think about the following questions:

a) What did you enjoy doing in your adolescent years?

b) What skills and abilities did you use in pursuing those interests? This could include good eye/hand coordination, logical thinking, loving a challenge, repetitive practice of a skill, or organising others.

c) How can you link those memories with what you are good at and what you enjoy doing today?

Working Years

In your working life you may have had to forego interests, activities, and experiences that you enjoyed in your younger years. Such interests are not dead, merely dormant. You can always take them up again, embellished with the experience of the intervening years.

An examination of why you work can tell you a lot about what drives you as a person, and what fulfils you. The driving forces behind your desire to work are much deeper than just being able to make money.

For example, if you are considering a change of career or even just of workplace, what do you enjoy in your present job that you would like to take forward into your next job?

Fulfilment may perhaps require no more than tweaking your current skills or situation.

Epilogue

We Are Part of a Natural World, Not Above It.

There I was in the midst of a beautiful park, birds busily making a life for themselves and perhaps for their young, trees rustling gently in the breeze, and a sense of peace that only nature can create.

Yet the more I listened, the more I heard, the more significant became the insignificant, and the more I saw what I didn't normally see.

In my daily life this was not a world of which I was a regular part. Life for me was the concrete jungle of hurrying people and, to quote the Australian poet Banjo Paterson, 'the ceaseless tramp of feet'.

Yet I was being inexorably drawn into this quiet, purposefulness going on around me. Each piece of this fascinating flora and fauna jigsaw had a part to play in creating a wonderfully colourful ecosystem, mutually supportive and working as one. I was almost forcibly reminded that I am a part of nature, not a foreigner or an interloper, and that I have a part to play in sustaining, nurturing, and harmonising this symphony of life.

I was surrounded by an aura of family—mother nature calling me home, welcoming me without judgment, putting loving arms around me, offering peace of mind, providing the resilience to cope with the winds and storms of life, and instilling a sense of compassion and understanding, even when she knew I had not always been loyal to her.

The peace of nature brought me back to the person I was born to be, endowed with a unique mix of talents, passions and potential, intended by Mother Nature, God, or whomever. A journey back in time, unearthing the 'me' I had once loved to be, reigniting desires left behind years ago that had remained unfulfilled, undeveloped, and unsatisfied.

The promise that only nature can bestow meant that these talents, passions, and desires were not dead, but merely dormant. Like green shoots rising from the ashes of a fire, they simply needed the gentle rains of my interest in order to sprout, grow strong, flourish, and blossom.

Take time out to go back to nature, to your roots and to your favourite habitats. Revisit, unearth, and rekindle your dormant passions and take your natural and rightful place in the ecology of human progress, development, and achievement.

Appendices

Appendix 1: The Manifesto

A MANIFESTO FOR ALLOWING EVERY PERSON'S NATURAL-BORN POTENTIAL TO BLOSSOM

Every person is born to enjoy their best life by developing their talents and following their passions to allow their natural potential to blossom.

The World

The realities of modern living are too often limiting people in their natural desire to find and become the person they were born to be.

In terms of Michelangelo's quote, "I saw the angel in the marble and carved until I set him free," the 'marble' represents peoples' 'imprisonment' within a 21st century way of life that requires people to live according to the expectations of an economic rationalist world.

To put the dollar ahead of the heart. The 'angel' is the self who yearns for the freedom to grow their natural gifts, allowing their unique potential to blossom.

The only person who can be the 'sculptor' is the individual, authentic inner self.

The role of society at all levels is to recognise, value, and extol the natural advantages and benefits of this approach as being essential to building a global environment of true, sustained human progress and achievement.

We live in a dramatically changing the world. Now is the time for a paradigm shift in our approach to personal development and human progress.

People

The Michelangelo quote, in today's terms, means freeing the true self within and allowing that self to feel accepted, publicly valued, and greatly wanted in this new emerging world.

Every person was born to be different. We each have

Appendix 1: The Manifesto

our own unique mix of gifts, talents, and passions. These give us all the basis of achieving a potential that is unachievable by anyone else.

Living the life we were born to enjoy entails becoming self-aware, valuing our unique individuality, and enjoying using and developing our natural-born abilities in our personal, business, and community lives.

The Law of Correspondence—one of the 12 Universal Laws—includes the statement "So within, so without." This advocates the need to bring our inner self and outer self together as the oneself. It also suggests that finding balance and happiness starts from the inside.

Freedom to develop one's abilities, talents, gifts, and passions would give each individual:

- *The enjoyment of learning with purpose*
- *The benefit of working with positive energy*
- *The ability to managing stress and building resilience*

- *A feeling of being engaged,*
- *A purpose centred on their creativity*
- *The opportunity to solve problems more easily*
- *A feeling of being closely connected*
- *Higher self-esteem, self-confidence, and self-belief*

What People Want

People want to be free to focus their lives on searching, discovering, and pursuing the purpose of their unique mix of natural abilities and interests.

Problem #1: Traditional thinking.

Today's perception of human progress and success is set solidly in the belief that:

- Paid work is the centre of life
- Economic development is the measure of success
- Enjoyment is not valued in work
- We identify ourselves by the job we have and the work we do
- Stress is a badge of honour

- We perceive retirement from work as retirement from life
- Doing what we enjoy has no place in the concept of hard work

An alternative philosophy is needed to better reflect the realities of this changing world.

Problem #2: Our Dependence on Artificial Living

We have turned the role of nature from being the centre of the world's health and wellbeing to becoming a slave to an economic hunger that devours all in its path.

For 10,000 years people based their lives around the use and development of their natural-born talents and gifts. Our connection and relationship to nature were the core of our way of living.

It's time to remember we are partners with nature, not its master.

Problem #3: The Future of Work

The place of work in peoples' lives is unclear. Power is increasingly in the hands of the worker as employees make their wishes known about key issues such as work flexibility, professional development, and mental health.

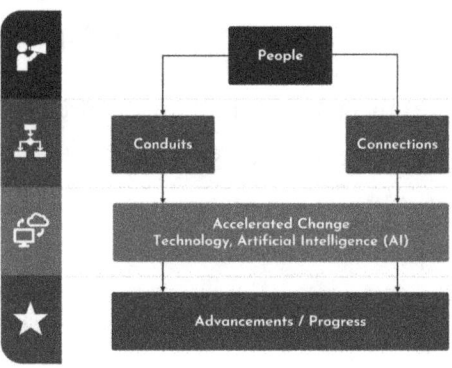

The Future of Work

Hierarchical structures within organisations are rapidly re-shaping, and in some cases flattening.

All of this adds credence to the recognition of the need to free the person within and allow their essential natural-born gifts to flow.

Appendix 1: The Manifesto

The diagram illustrates that people will always want:

- Structures within which people can collaborate to achieve a purpose
- Connections with positive, like-minded people to share and achieve outcomes of common interest
- Effective management of change, including the growth of Artificial Intelligence

The aim is to advance human progress in a way that improves people's wellbeing.

The Solution

The Principle of Life Development reflects the desire to:

- Maximise corporate and global development based on the use and development of peoples' natural abilities in all areas of life, not just at work
- Create greater harmony between personal development and professional development

What This Can Mean For The Individual

The basics for achieving this are for each person to become aware of their unique gifts and passions, and to enjoy using and developing these gifts and passions in all aspects of their personal, business, and community lives. People want to feel accepted, publicly valued and wanted for their natural abilities.

What This Can Mean For Business

Businesses, particularly senior managers, would quickly recognise the potential of these sorts of benefits in the workplace:

- Productivity would boom,
- Mental health issues would be reduced,
- Stress would be limited to the 'positive stress' of good business
- Conflicts would be reduced
- A higher quality of output would be achieved through teamwork
- There would be a greater blending of personal and corporate goals, which would improve staff stability

- There would be an improvement in attracting the right staff to the right jobs

The effect would spread throughout the business world, to governments and other influencers of public policy and opinion.

The Global Dream

21st century communication technology has been drawing the people, communities, businesses, and countries of the world closer together. Daily issues of concern, ideas for improvement, and views on what works or doesn't work travel at speed throughout today's fast-paced world.

People all over the world are realising 'we are all in this together'.

This is causing people everywhere to stop and reflect on what's important in the life of humanity, irrespective of culture, colour, or creed.

Now is the time to turn our minds to what naturally drives our thinking, our lives, and our desires for true progress.

Appendix 2: Tips for Keeping You Mentally Fit

You know what you can do to stay physically fit, but what can you do to stay mentally fit?

Here are some useful, positive indicators of the extent to which you can demonstrate mental health and wellness.

Keeping mentally fit does not automatically mean being physically active, even though health professionals generally focus on 'getting physical'. The key focus needs to be *enjoyment* of whatever you do, be it physical, mental, social or spiritual. Physical activity will only benefit your mental fitness if you enjoy the activity. If you don't enjoy it, you won't be doing it for long.

The tips shown here are not new... it's their relationship to and impact on the desire to stay mentally fit for the rest of your life that gives them their power and significance.

Appendix 2: Tips for Keeping You Mentally Fit

- Have at least one passionate interest outside of work, especially one that is creative and preferably non-competitive. Examples include music, arts, genealogy, and photography. If your preference is a competitive interest, ensure that fun is a big part of the experience. The idea is to renew your emotional energy.
- Mix with positive, like-minded people with whom you share a non-work creative interest
- Having an array of complementary-opposite interests such as:
    o Indoor and outdoor.
    o Using your hands and using your mind.
    o Participating in solo activities and in group activities.
    o Spending time in environments that are quiet and in environments that are noisy.
- Create a harmonious life mix of energising interests that sustain energy-draining demands.

- Have at least one non-work interest principally because it makes you feel good about yourself.
- Have multiple, diverse social networks.
- Take pride in yourself. This includes your diet, appearance, and what you say.
- Look to continuously improve yourself.
- Be kind to yourself.
- Believe you have an abundant life.
- Feel you have adequate control over your life decisions.
- Do things that help other people feel better.
- Know and develop those abilities that other people value in you.
- Love what you have and what you have achieved.
- Having an attitude of gratitude for the good things that happen in your life.
- Being aware of your senses and what is going on around you.
- Imagine you can step outside of yourself and watch yourself in action. Take notice of any

circumstances in which you see yourself as particularly stressed or particularly at peace with yourself. Decide that you are going to be aware of such circumstances in future and the effect they have on your mental health.

End Notes

1. "World Population Prospects, 2019", United Nations statement, 2019

2. Gwen Meyer, Incremental Steps Pty Ltd, Adelaide

3. "An ageing workforce isn't a burden. It's an opportunity", World Economic Forum (www.weforum.org)

4. "Maintaining Passion, Enthusiasm, Motivation, Momentum", Charles Kovess: Australia's Passion Provocateur, Melbourne

About the Author

Peter Nicholls

Peter Nicholls worked in the development of leisure and recreation opportunities for people of all ages and backgrounds. Those years taught him much about the benefits of enjoyment to health and wellbeing, personal development, and work/life harmony.

Dealings with influential authorities were, however, frustratingly difficult. Work was king and recreation simply 'fluffy stuff' for which funding and other public support was seen as being of low importance.

His encore career as a Life Enjoyment Mentor has given him the opportunity to evolve a core message:

When you lose yourself in any interest that you enjoy, you find yourself

Since 2003, he has broadened his experience, knowledge, insight, and perspective. The impact of basing one's life around enjoyment can go so deep as to help answer life's fundamental question, 'Why are we here?'

Peter's Expertise

Peter's natural skills include the ability to listen in order to hear what is not being said, to listen without judgement, to be impartial about any the issues his clients are facing, and to not place his own values on anything the client says.

As Gary Edwards, National President of Professional Speakers Australia, said of Peter Nicholls, "Peter is very skilled at being able to identify connections between what I enjoyed then and what I am good at now… and why."

His central program, called simply 'Enjoy Being You', offers a structure that takes you back to the basics of what has always given you enjoyment throughout your life to date.

From this, we bring to light the natural abilities used and developed through those interests. This creates a positive foundation on which you can build the future you will enjoy living—including life after leaving work.

The program centres on the Seven Keys to Enjoying Being Your True Self:

The 7 Keys to Enjoying Being Your True Self

Any one of the seven keys can trigger the other six keys, and the outcome of them all is greater than the sum of the individual parts.

As C. Harris, one of his clients in Adelaide, South Australia, said of the course, "I would recommend your course to anyone, no matter what problems in life they face. It was great to just realise that Life is a true gift."

www.ingramcontent.com/pod-product-compliance
Lightning Source LLC
LaVergne TN
LVHW052255070426
835507LV00035B/2904